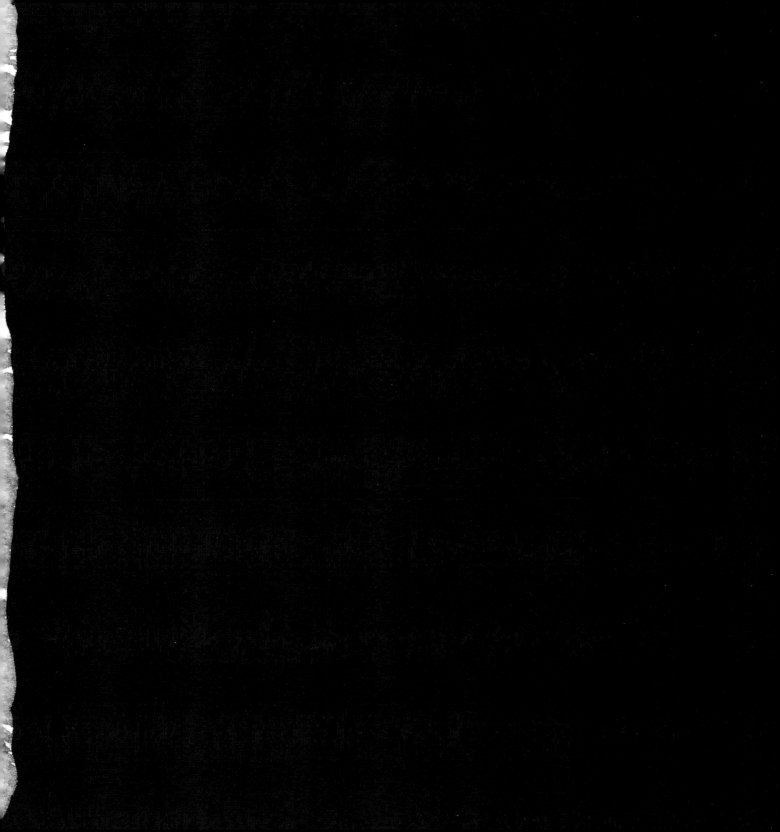

ISBN 1-86958-143-1

© Anne Geddes 1995

Published by Moa Beckett Publishers Limited,
28 Poland Road, Glenfield, Auckland, P O Box 100-749,
North Shore Mail Centre, Auckland 1330, New Zealand.

Designed by Jane Seabrook
Produced by Kel Geddes
Colour separations by HQ Imaging
Typesetting by Advision
Printed through Colorcraft, Hong Kong

ANNE GEDDES

A

Angel

B

Bee

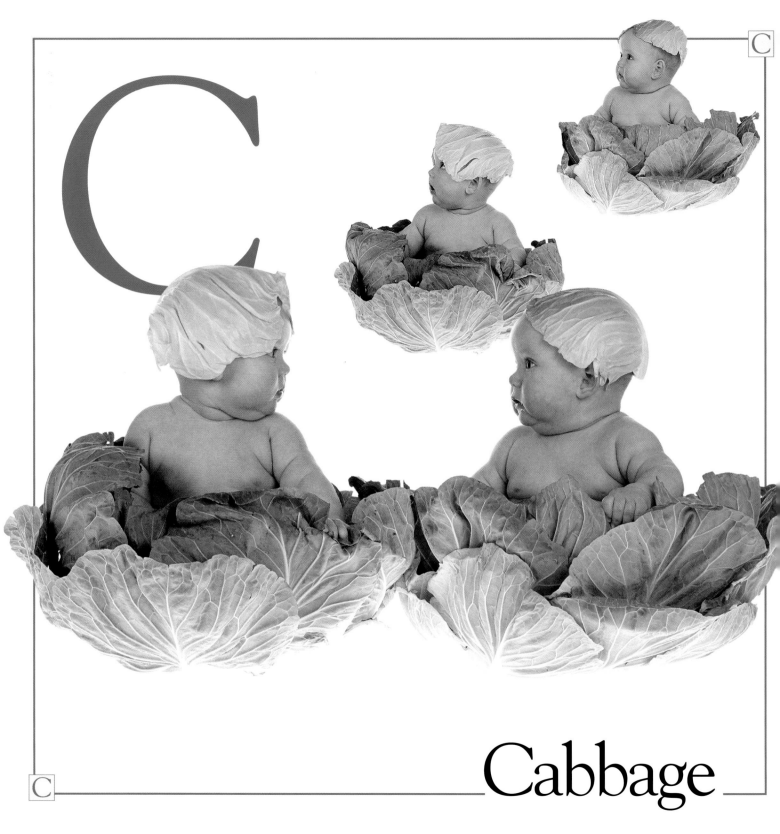

C

Cabbage

D

Duck

E

Egg

F

Fairy

G

Grandad

H

Hat

I

Inside

J

Jack-in-a-box

K

Kiss

L

Lily

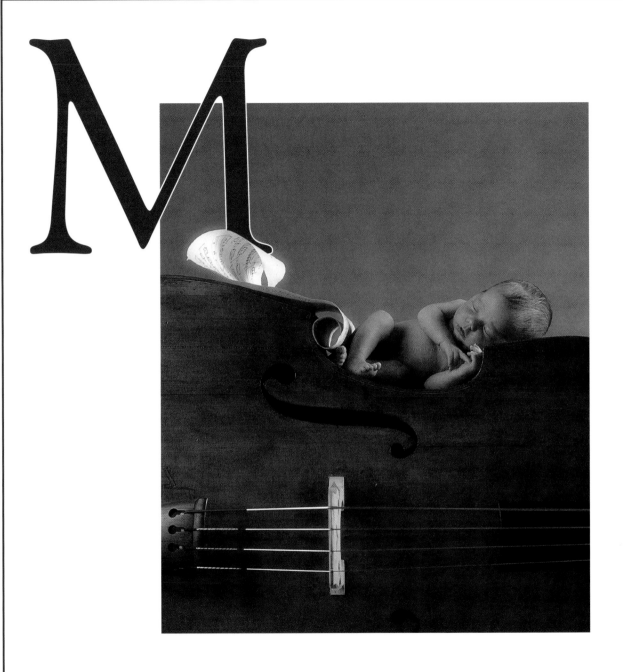

M

Music

N

Nest

Oh no!

P

Pumpkin

P

Q

Queen

R

R

Rose

S

Sunflower

T

Tulip

U

Upside-down

V

Valentine

V

V

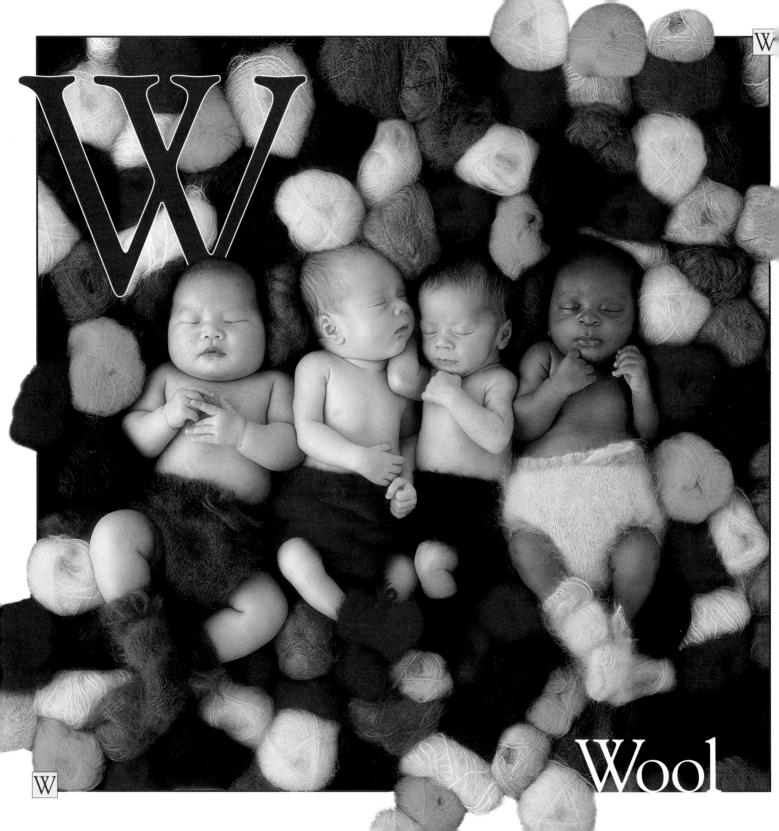

W

Wool

X

Xmas

Y

Yawn

Z

Zzzzz

Z

Z